ॐ

HOMA

Science and Practice

Ashwini Kumar Aggarwal

जय गुरुदेव

ISBN13: 978-81-945212-8-0   Paperback Edition (Black/White)
ISBN13: 978-81-945212-9-7   Hardbound Edition (Full Color)
ISBN13: 978-81-946008-0-0   Digital Edition (Full Color)

Title: **Homa Science and Practice**
Author: **Ashwini Kumar Aggarwal**

Printed and Published by
Devotees of Sri Sri Ravi Shankar Ashram
34 Sunny Enclave, Devigarh Road
Patiala 147001, Punjab, India

https://advaita56.weebly.com/
The Art of Living Centre

https://www.artofliving.org/

21st February 2020 Maha Shivaratri Rudra Puja at Sunny Enclave
Showers of Grace, Sweetness of Pancamrit, 108 Blissful Participants.

KrishnaPaksh Trayodashi, Phalgun, Vasant Ritu, Shravan Nakshatra
Vikram Samvat 2076 Paridhavi, Saka Era 1941 Vikari

1st Edition February 2020

जय गुरुदेव

Sri Sri Ravi Shankar

havan ~ shraddha strong faith ~ shat sampatti

Blessing

All that you can do is to raise the level of Sattva. And then when Sattva's level is high, we have to wait one moment, any moment knowledge can dawn there.

All that you can do to have sunlight in this room, is to open the curtains and keep the windows open. And when dawn comes, it just dawns. You have the sunlight inside.

Sri Sri Ravi Shankar
A discourse on Yogasara Upanishad

Oct 2005. Navratri Homa Gujarat Ashram

Contents

Prayer

शान्तिपाठः

ॐ सह नाववतु । सह नौ भुनक्तु । सह वीर्यं करवावहै ।
तेजस्वि नावधीतमस्तु मा विद्विषावहै ॥
ॐ शान्तिः शान्तिः शान्तिः ॥

oṃ saha nāvavatu | saha nau bhunaktu | saha

vīryaṃ karavāvahai | tejasvi nāvadhītamastu mā

vidviṣāvahai ‖ oṃ śānti śānti śāntiḥ ‖

Peace Invocation
O Pure Loving Grace!

May we be taken care of along with family and friends.
May we enjoy socializing and eating together.
May we support each other's vision and growth.
May our intellect accept new ideas and changing trends.
May we spend more time in praise than not, may we talk
of each other's virtues rather than harp otherwise.

Peace in our heart, in our body and in our environs.

Preface

Homa or Havan or Yajna as it is popularly called, is a practice of engaging the community. By this, families can come together and partake of Vedic Wisdom.

A havan is a simple enjoyable technique, nay a fundamental ritual that helps elevate the consciousness. It fosters peace and harmony. It purifies the basic elements, viz. earth, water and air. It can prevent natural or manmade upheavals.

Yajna can give the right direction to children and bring to fore their hidden talents. It can give insights to parents and society leaders on what can be done to make their commune harmonious, self-reliant, and prosperous.

A havan can be performed all alone initially, and in due course many people can join in as its beatitude spreads. Alone it can be done in a matter of a few minutes, and in a well-sized congregation it can take from one to four hours.

Homa gives the maximum benefit when the pace is sensible, there is an air of relaxed naturalness, young children are involved, and couples join in.

Singing and **Meditation** and a **hearty Meal** make the Yajna supremely divine. It is a hallowed tradition that is followed in many parts of the world and finds mention in the earliest scriptures.

Here is given a simple method that may be followed by anyone, anywhere, anytime.

Agnihotra Homa अग्निहोत्र

Honoring the fire in creation,
the one within and the one without.
    Honoring the light in creation,
    the one within and the one without.

agni surya – अग्निः सूर्यः

the heat = digestive fire within,
and the energy without which keeps everything going.
the light = light of awareness within,
and the sunlight that awakens us all.

Agnihotra is done **exactly** at sunset or at sunrise by
noting the time specific to your place.

Clean the area. Have a shower and wear fresh clothes.

0. Arrange the havan-kund and light the fire. Here use:
- Copper pot – a havankund of specific dimensions.
- Dried cow dung cakes of desi gobar (A2 cow).
- Desi-cow A2 ghee.
- Unbroken rice grains (preferably unpolished).
- Time Chart to the exact second for your place.
- Light the fire **without** using camphor. Simply dip a
  piece of cowdung-cake in ghee and hold it in a diya
  flame till it catches fire, then put this in the
  havankund.

1. It consists of two offerings in all.

Notes:

If we do this havan daily,

- It is not needed to wash the pyramid each time
- We can also align the pyramid in the same manner each time, i.e. keep the dot to EAST
- Sit facing East if convenient
- The copper pyramid is of specific size and without handles
- After the havan, sit for a few minutes in contemplation
- The pyramid will be hot, so use a pair of tongs or a handkerchief to move it

<u>Copper Pyramid Dimensions</u>

Top square = 16 cm x 16 cm = 6.3 in x 6.3 in
Bottom square = 6 cm x 6 cm = 2.36 in x 2.36 in
Height =
      Inner = 6.5 cm = 2.6 in
      Outer = 6.8 cm = 2.7 in (due to thickness of
      copper sheet).
Thickness of copper sheet = 0.3 cm = 0.1 in

<u>Evening Agnihotra Chant</u>
<u>(to the exact second at Sunset in your area)</u>

Offer a mix of rice-and-ghee to the fire while saying svaha. It is only twice.

अग्नये स्वाहा । अग्नये इदं न मम ।
agnaye svāhā | agnaye idaṃ na mama |

प्रजापतये स्वाहा । प्रजापतये इदं न मम ।
prajāpataye svāhā | prajāpataye idaṃ na mama |

7:22pm 11 June 2012 Evening Agnihotra, Punjabi Bagh

<u>Morning Agnihotra Chant</u>
<u>(to the exact second at Sunrise in your area)</u>

Offer a mix of rice-and-ghee to the fire while saying svaha. It is only twice.

सूर्याय स्वाहा । सूर्याय इदं न मम ।
sūryāya svāhā । sūryāya idaṃ na mama ।

प्रजापतये स्वाहा । प्रजापतये इदं न मम ।
prajāpataye svāhā । prajāpataye idaṃ na mama ।

Morning Agnihotra, Mediterranean Sea beach

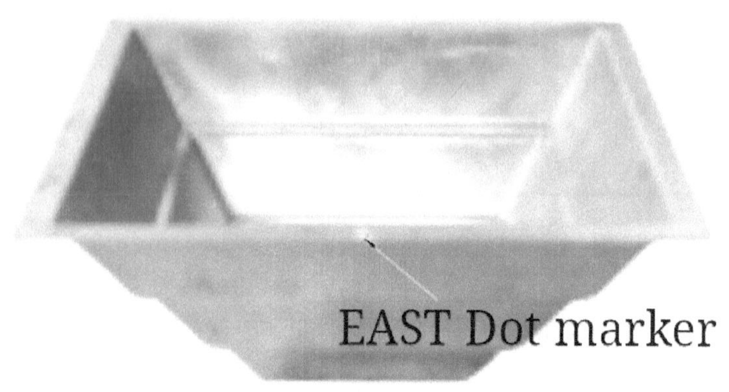
EAST Dot marker

<u>Agnihotra Necessary Items</u>

1. Copper Pyramid

2. Copper Stand for Pyramid

Place the Pyramid on Stand to avoid heating the floor

3. Copper Tongs for moving Pyramid or adjusting cowdung cakes

4. Copper spoon for taking ghee

5. Copper dish for holding ghee

The Copper Kit

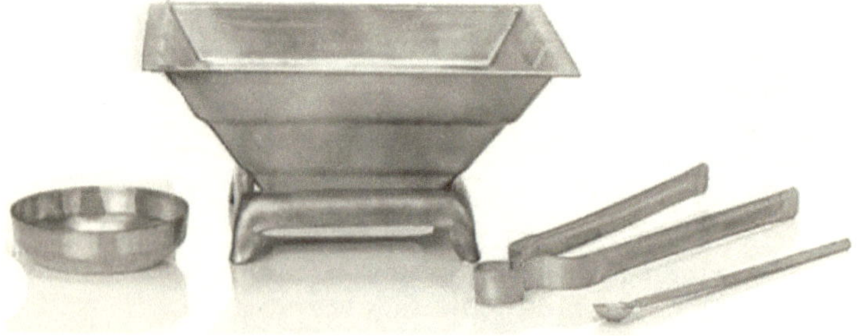

6. Unbroken Rice grains

7. Desi Cow Ghee A2

8. Dried Cowdung Cakes

9. Time Chart with seconds accuracy for your location

Agnihotra Timings 2020

Location: Patiala, Punjab 147001, India
Timezone: Asia/Calcutta, Latitude: 30°20'23", Longitude: 76°23'12"

D		January				February	
		Rise	Set			Rise	Set
M							
T							
W	01	07:25:28	17:30:43				
T	02	07:25:42	17:31:26				
F	03	07:25:53	17:32:11				
S	04	07:26:03	17:32:56	01	07:19:24	17:56:58	
S	05	07:26:12	17:33:42	02	07:18:47	17:57:50	
M	06	07:26:18	17:34:29	03	07:18:09	17:58:42	
T	07	07:26:23	17:35:16	04	07:17:29	17:59:34	
W	08	07:26:27	17:36:05	05	07:16:47	18:00:26	
T	09	07:26:28	17:36:53	06	07:16:05	18:01:17	
F	10	07:26:28	17:37:43	07	07:15:21	18:02:08	
S	11	07:26:26	17:38:33	08	07:14:35	18:02:59	
S	12	07:26:22	17:39:23	09	07:13:49	18:03:49	
M	13	07:26:17	17:40:14	10	07:13:01	18:04:39	
T	14	07:26:10	17:41:05	11	07:12:12	18:05:29	

28 Feb 2013 Havan celebrating Dipanshu's Birthday

Maha Mrityunjaye Havan महामृत्युंजय

Clean the area. Have a shower and wear fresh clothes.
0. Arrange the havan-kund and light the fire.
1. Invoke Guru Tattva by chanting

ॐ श्री गुरुभ्यो नमः । हरिः ॐ ॥

oṃ śrī gurubhyo namaḥ । hariḥ oṃ ॥

2. Invoke Ganesha by chanting

ॐ महागणपतये नमः ।

वक्रतुण्ड महाकाय सूर्यकोटिसमप्रभ ।

निर्विघ्नं कुरु मे देव सर्वकार्येषु सर्वदा ॥

oṃ mahāgaṇapataye namaḥ ।

vakratuṇḍa mahākāya

sūryakoṭisamaprabha । nirvighnaṃ kuru

me deva sarvakāryeṣu sarvadā ॥

3. Start offering ghee/samagri while chanting

ॐ त्र्यम्बकं यजामहे सुगन्धिं पुष्टिवर्धनम् ।

उर्वारुकमिव बन्धनान् मृत्योर् मुक्षीय माऽमृतात् ॥

स्वाहा । oṃ tryambakaṃ yajāmahe

sugandhiṃ puṣṭivardhanam ।

urvārukamiva bandhanān mṛtyor mukṣīya

mā'mṛtāt ॥ svāhā ।

We may chant for few minutes say 11 minutes, or for a specific count, say 21 times. Then relax and sit in deep contemplation for some time. Finally take a couple of slow deep breaths. Open your eyes with a loving smile.

4. Ending chant – a prayer of your choice

लोकाः समस्ताः सुखिनो भवन्तु ॥

lokā samastā sukhino bhavantu ॥ x 3

5. Shanti mantra

ॐ शान्तिः शान्तिः शान्तिः ॥

oṃ śāntiḥ śāntiḥ śāntiḥ ॥

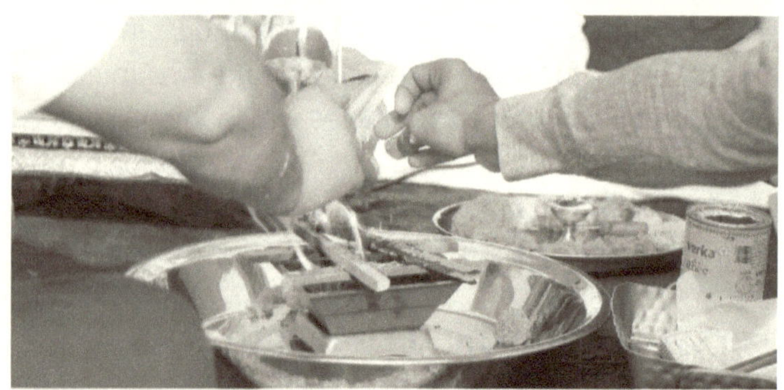

Vyahriti Homa व्याहृति

Honoring the three geographical planes in creation:
Bhu Bhuva Suva – भूः भुवः स्वः
the earth, the intervening atmospheric space, the
celestial regions.

Vyahriti homa consists of 4 offerings in all.

Clean the area. Have a shower and wear fresh clothes.

0. Arrange the havan-kund and light the fire.

1. Chant

भूः स्वाहा । अग्नये इदं न मम ।

bhūḥ svāhā । agnaye idaṃ na mama ।

offer a spoon of ghee/ havan samagri while saying svaha.

2. Chant

भुवः स्वाहा । वायवे इदं न मम ।

bhuvaḥ svāhā । vāyave idaṃ na mama ।

offer a spoon of ghee/ havan samagri while saying svaha.

3. Chant

स्वः स्वाहा । सूर्याय इदं न मम ।

svaḥ svāhā । sūryāya idaṃ na mama ।

offer a spoon of ghee/ havan samagri while saying svaha.

4. Chant

भूः भुवः स्वः स्वाहा । प्रजापतये इदं न मम ।

bhūḥ bhuvaḥ svaḥ svāhā । prajāpataye

idaṃ na mama ।

offer a spoon of ghee/ havan samagri while saying svaha.

<u>**Chanting Notes:**</u>

Vedic chanting follows Sandhi - Panini Sanskrit grammar principles. **This makes the actual chant sound like:**

भूस् स्वाहा । अग्रये इदं न मम ।
bhūs svāhā | agnaye idaṃ na mama |

भुवस् स्वाहा । वायवे इदं न मम ।
bhuvas svāhā | vāyave idaṃ na mama |

स्वस् स्वाहा । सूर्याय इदं न मम ।
svas svāhā | sūryāya idaṃ na mama |

भूर् भुवस् स्वस् स्वाहा । प्रजापतये इदं न मम ।
bhūr bhuvas svas svāhā | prajāpataye idaṃ na mama |

Havan to celebrate occasions and make any get-together joyous, blissful, meaningful

0 Fixing the Date and Time and Venue
1c. List of Participants, Invitees
1a. Preparation of Venue
1b. Preparation of Self - body, mind, heart
2 Arrangement of Puja Items
3 Pranayama
4 Gayatri Japa
5 Om Namah Shivaya Chanting
Affirmation that I am whole and complete
6 Guru Puja
7 Havan
Affirmation I am nothing
8 Meditation
9 Shanti Mantras and Blessings
10 Satsang
11 Aarti as Satsang continues
12 Prasadam – a delicious meal offered with honor to all

Arrangement of Puja Items

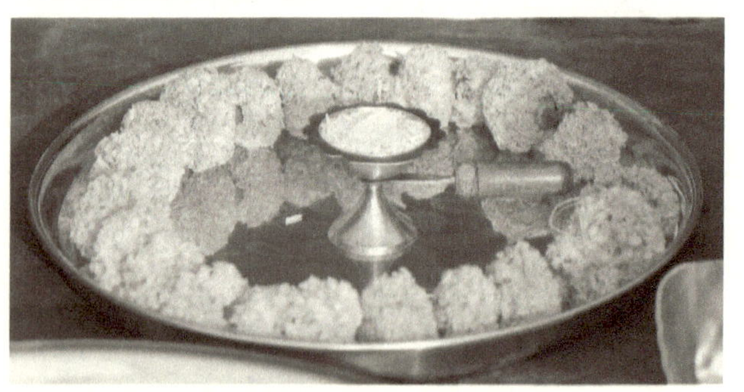

Pranayama

Gayatri Japa

Om Namah Shivaya slow chant pranayama in clear and
loud voice
(We may chant 5 times or 11 times or for a few minutes.)

Meditation

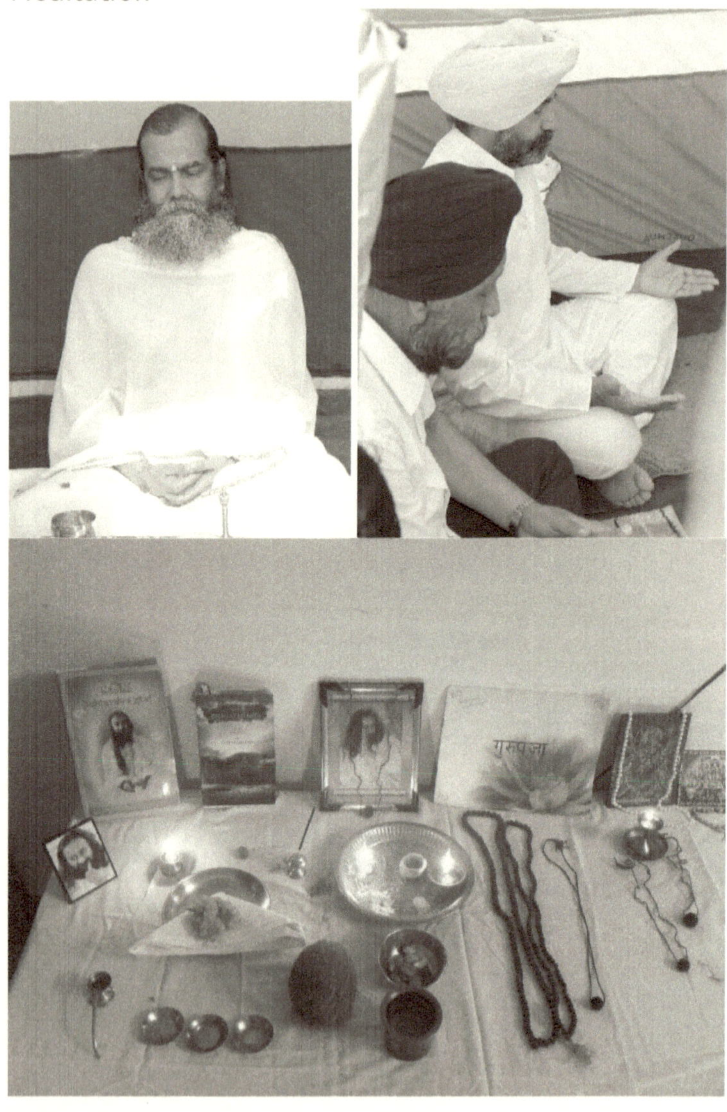

ॐ स्वस्तिः प्रजाभ्यᳵ परिपालयन्ताम् । न्यायेन मार्गेण महीं
महीशाः । गो ब्राह्मणेभ्यः शुभमस्तु नित्यम् ।
लोकाः समस्ताः सुखिनो भवन्तु ॥ काले वर्षतु पर्जन्यः पृथिवी
सस्यशालिनी । देशोऽयं क्षोभरहितः ब्राह्मणाः सन्तु निर्भयाः ॥
सर्वे भवन्तु सुखिनः । सर्वे सन्तु निरामयाः ।
सर्वे भद्राणि पश्यन्तु । मा कश्चिद् दुःखभाग् भवेत् ॥
असतो मा सद् गमय । तमसो मा ज्योतिर् गमय ।
मृत्योर् मा अमृतं गमय ॥
ॐ पूर्णमदः पूर्णमिदं पूर्णात् पूर्णमुदच्यते ।
पूर्णस्य पूर्णमादाय पूर्णमेवावशिष्यते ॥
ॐ शान्तिः शान्तिः शान्तिः ॥

oṃ svastiḥ prajābhyaᳵ paripālayantām ।

nyāyena mārgeṇa mahīṃ mahīśāḥ । go

brāhmaṇebhyaḥ śubhamastu nityam । lokāḥ

samastāḥ sukhino bhavantu ॥ kāle varṣatu

parjanyaḥ pṛthivī sasyaśālinī । deśo'yaṃ

kṣobharahitaḥ brāhmaṇāḥ santu nirbhayāḥ ॥

sarve bhavantu sukhinaḥ । sarve santu

nirāmayāḥ । sarve bhadrāṇi paśyantu । mā

kaścid duḥkhabhāg bhavet ॥ asato mā sad

gamaya । tamaso mā jyotir gamaya ।

mṛtyor mā amṛtaṃ gamaya ||
oṃ pūrṇamadaḥ pūrṇamidaṃ pūrṇāt
pūrṇamudacyate | pūrṇasya pūrṇamādāya
pūrṇamevāvaśiṣyate || oṃ śāntiḥ śāntiḥ śāntiḥ
||

Aarti

दीप आरती

न तत्र सूर्यो भाति न चन्द्रतारकं नेमा विद्युतो भान्ति कुतोऽयमग्निः । तमेव भान्तम् अनुभाति सर्वं तस्य भासा सर्वमिदं विभाति ॥

कर्पूर आरती

कर्पूरगौरं करुणावतारं संसारसारं भुजगेन्द्रहारम् । सदा वसन्तं हृदयारविन्दे भवंभवानी सहितं नमामि ॥

dīpa āratī

na tatra sūryo bhāti na candratārakam nemā
vidyuto bhānti kuto'yamagniḥ | tameva
bhāntam anubhāti sarvaṃ tasya bhāsā
sarvamidaṃ vibhāti ||

karpūra āratī

karpūragauraṃ karuṇāvatāraṃ saṃsārasāraṃ
bhujagendrahāram | sadā vasantaṃ
hradayāravinde bhavaṃbhavānī sahitaṃ
namāmi ||

Prasadam – Delicious meal served with honor to all

Havan Kund – Pots for doing Havan

Iron Havan Kund from Gayatri Parivar

Copper Havan Kund with handles

Iron Havan Kund

Clay Havan Kund

Agnihotra Pyramid

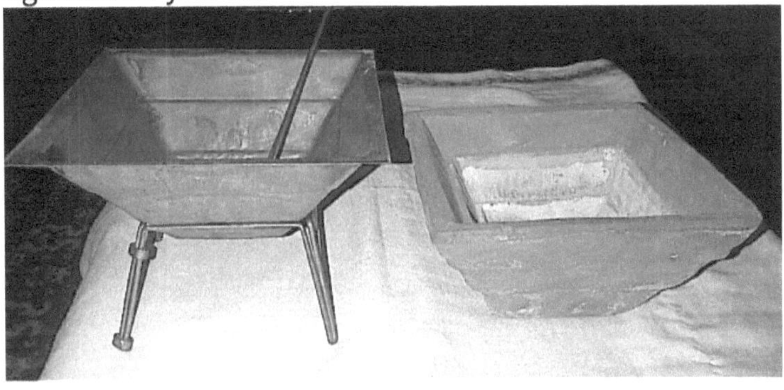

Bricks Vedi

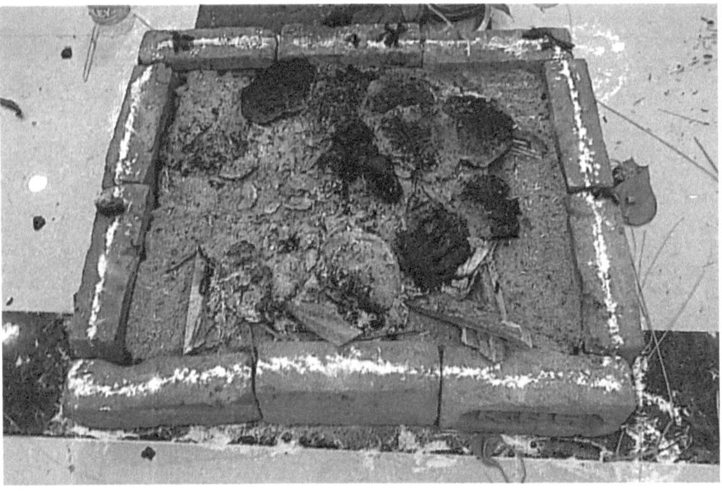

Vedic rituals, Garhapatya (circular), Dakshinagni (semi circle) and Ahavaniya (square)

Shrikant Jichkar home, Nagpur

Maheshwar, Indore

Verses from Scriptures indicating Homa

<u>Bhagavad Gita 4th chapter, 16th chapter</u>

ब्रह्मार्पणं ब्रह्म हविः , ब्रह्माग्नौ ब्रह्मणा हुतम् । ब्रह्मैव तेन गन्तव्यम् , ब्रह्मकर्मसमाधिना ॥

brahmārpaṇaṁ brahma haviḥ , brahmāgnau brahmaṇā

hutam | brahmaiva tena gantavyam ,

brahmakarmasamādhinā || 4.24

Perform each **offering** as the supreme Lord's will. Calmly notice in all situations and persons his direct presence. **Bhagavad Gita 4.24**

अभयं सत्त्वसंशुद्धिः , ज्ञानयोगव्यवस्थितिः ।

दानं दमश्च यज्ञश्च , स्वाध्यायस् तप आर्जवम् ॥

abhayaṁ sattvasaṁśuddhiḥ , jñānayogavyavasthitiḥ |

dānaṁ damaśca yajñaśca , svādhyāyas tapa ārjavam ||

16.1

Fearlessness in general, Sattva solidified, Steadfastness in Thought and Deed, Social Service, Self Restraint in times of difficulty, **Giving oblations to fire**, practice of Self Study, Enduring discipline willingly and Sincerity. **Bhagavad Gita 16.1**

यस्य अग्निहोत्रम् अदर्शम् अपौर्णमासम् अचातुर्मास्यम् अनाग्रयणम् अतिथिवर्जितं च । अहुतम् अवैश्वदेवम् अविधिना हुतम् आसप्तमान् तस्य लोकान् हिनस्ति ॥

yasya **agnihotram** adarśam apaurṇamāsam acāturmāsyam anāgrayaṇam atithivarjitaṃ ca | ahutam avaiśvadevam avidhinā hutam āsaptamān tasya lokān hinasti || **Mundaka 1.2.3**

Mummy Papa 50th marriage anniversary Golden Jubilee celebrations

References

https://homatherapyindia.com/
https://agnihotralife.com/ https://homatherapy.org/

https://play.google.com/store/apps/details?id=app.gah
omatherapy.agnihotramitra&hl=en_IN
https://play.google.com/store/apps/details?id=com.ma
dhavashram.agnihotratimetable&hl=en_IN

https://agnihotra.vishwaglobal.com/
https://vaidicpujas.org/navratri/

https://www.awgp.org/en/literature/book/procedure_o
f_gayatri_yagya/v8.2

Checklist for Guru Puja
3 types of fruits, two betel leaves and a betel nut,
garlands, loose flowers, white hankerchief, rice grains,
ganga-jal, chandan, dhoop, ghee-diya, camphor aarti,
wooden-stool for placing puja items.

Checklist for Havan
Havan kund, desi ghee, dried mango sticks, dried
cowdung cakes, camphor, matchbox, bowl and spoon,
pancapatra.

Epilogue

Once in a blue moon the magical Ships Sail, leaving a wake of exciting currents. If you are lucky, a bit of the magic touches your countenance, and tangents you over to Supreme Grace.

सर्वे भवन्तु सुखिनः । सर्वे सन्तु निरामयाः ।

सर्वे भद्राणि पश्यन्तु । मा कश्चिद् दुःख भाग्भवेत् ॥

ॐ शान्तिः शान्तिः शान्तिः ॥

When faith has blossomed in life,
Every step is led by the Divine.

Sri Sri Ravi Shankar

Om Namah Shivaya

जय गुरुदेव

9:07pm 17 Oct 2007. Chandi Homa Gujarat Ashram